MANIFESTOS FOR THE 21ST CENTURY

SERIES EDITORS: URSULA OWEN AND JUDITH VIDAL-HALL

This series began with free expression as its
central theme, arising at a time when the
problems of censorship and offence were very
much centre stage. As it has developed over the
years the Manifesto series has expanded to
include questions of rights, liberties, tolerance,
silencing, dissent and other major issues of our
day. The distinguished authors, some of the
world's sharpest analysts and foremost thinkers,
address a wide range of themes, from trust to
equality, from multiculturalism to the Israel–
Palestine conflict, from the condition of Europe
to the nature of offence.

We live in a world where people with widely
different cultural habits and beliefs live in
proximity, where words, images and behaviour
come under the closest scrutiny and are fiercely
debated. In such a complex and precarious
world, these books aim to surprise, clarify and
provoke in equal measure.

MANIFESTOS FOR THE 21ST CENTURY

MULTICULTURALISM AND ITS DISCONTENTS

Rethinking Diversity after 9/11

KENAN MALIK

LONDON NEW YORK CALCUTTA

Seagull Books, 2013

© Kenan Malik, 2013

ISBN 978 0 85742 1 142

British Library Cataloguing-in-Publication Data
A catalogue record for this book is available
from the British Library

Typeset and designed by Seagull Books, Calcutta, India
Printed and bound by Hyam Enterprises, Calcutta, India

ACKNOWLEDGEMENTS

The ideas and arguments in this book have developed through more than two decades of debates, discussions and disagreements, public and private. Many of the themes have been adapted from essays and papers I have written and speeches I have given over that time, in particular 'Making a Difference: Culture, Race and Social Policy', published in *Patterns of Prejudice* in 2005, and 'What's Wrong with Multiculturalism? A European Perspective', my 2012 Milton K. Wong lecture in Vancouver. Parts of this essay have also been adapted from my books *Strange Fruit: Why Both Sides Are Wrong in the Race Debate* (2008) and *From Fatwa to Jihad: The Rushdie Affair and Its Legacy* (2009).

1

On 22 July 2011, Anders Behring Breivik planted a car bomb outside government buildings in the Regjeringskvartalet area of Oslo. The explosion killed eight people and injured more than 200. Two hours later, Breivik, dressed in an all-black paramilitary uniform, launched an attack on a summer camp organized by the youth division of the Norwegian Labour Party on the nearby island of Utoya. For an hour and a half, he walked round the campsite, firing indiscriminately with machine guns, unzipping tents and gunning down people cowering inside. Sixty-nine people were killed in the homicidal rampage.

It was a viscerally shocking moment, the worst atrocity that Norway had suffered since the Second World War. Breivik's aim was to launch not simply a physical assault but an existential one, too. In his eyes the killings in Oslo and Utoya were the first shots in a war to defend Europe against multiculturalism. Shortly before the attacks, he had published online a 1,500-page manifesto entitled *2083: A European Declaration of Independence*. '2083' refers to the four hundredth anniversary of the Battle of Vienna when the advance of the Ottoman Empire into Europe had been checked by the armies of the Habsburg Empire. Twenty-first-century Europe, Breivik claimed, faced a similar threat and required a similar military response. 'The individuals I have been accused of illegally executing,' he wrote, 'are supporters of the anti-European hate ideology known as multiculturalism, an ideology that facilitates Islamization and Islamic demographic warfare.' They were 'killed in self defence through a pre-emptive

strike' having 'been found guilty and condemned to death'.[1]

Few but the most psychopathic could
have any sympathy for Breivik's homicidal
frenzy. Yet, the belief that multiculturalism
is undermining Western civilization, that
Muslim immigration is eroding the social
and cultural fabric of European societies,
transforming Europe into 'Eurabia', that
politicians responsible for allowing this to
happen are at best irresponsible, at worst
traitors—all these notions now find a widespread hearing, and not just on the fringes
of politics. Bruce Bawer is a distinguished US
literary critic and poet. He was, he wrote in
the *Wall Street Journal*, outraged by Breivik's
attack, not simply because of the carnage, but
because the carnage would 'deal a heavy blow
to an urgent cause'. Breivik's rampage was
'unspeakably evil' and yet, claimed Bawer, he
was expressing in his manifesto 'a legitimate
concern about genuine problems'. There is,
wrote Bawer, 'reason to be deeply concerned

about all these things and to want to see them addressed forcefully by government leaders'.[2] British writer and broadcaster Melanie Phillips is a recipient of Britain's highest accolade for political journalism, the Orwell Prize, and a fellow panellist of mine on BBC Radio 4's weekly debate programme *The Moral Maze*. She, like Bawer, condemned the 'horrible carnage' at Utoya. She, too, insisted that 'Multiculturalism and Islamic extremism raise entirely legitimate and very serious concerns about defending a culture from attack both from within and from without.'[3]

Twenty years ago, multiculturalism was widely seen as the answer to many of Europe's social problems. *We're All Multiculturalists Now*, as American sociologist Nathan Glazer, a former critic of pluralism, suggested in the title of his book. Celebration of difference, respect for pluralism, avowal of identity politics had all come to be regarded as the hallmarks of a progressive, anti-racist outlook and as the foundation of modern liberal democracies.

And yet, the very moment that Glazer was declaring us all to be multiculturalists was also the moment that many stopped being so. Or, rather, it was the moment when doubts about multiculturalism began to haunt mainstream politics, particularly in Europe. Over the past decade, and particularly in the wake of the 9/11 attacks, such doubts have grown and come to dominate the debate. Today, multiculturalism is seen by growing numbers of people not as the solution to but as the cause of Europe's myriad social ills. That perception has led mainstream politicians, such as British prime minister David Cameron, German chancellor Angela Merkel and former French president Nicolas Sarkozy, to denounce the dangers of multiculturalism. It has provided fuel for the success of far-right parties and populist politicians across Europe from Geert Wilders in the Netherlands to Marine Le Pen in France, from the True Finns to the UK Independence Party. And it greased the obscene, homicidal rampage of Anders Behring Breivik.

The reasons for this transformation in the perception of multiculturalism are complex and at the heart of what I will explore in this book. It is not just the perception of multiculturalism that has changed but also the character of its critique. As much of the debate surrounding the Breivik assault reveals, the contemporary critique is often driven by crude notions—indeed myths— about Islam, Muslims, immigration, European history and Western values.

These changes pose a problem in writing a book such as this. I have been critical of multiculturalism from long before it was fashionable to be so. But my critique is rooted in a completely different vision from that of most contemporary opponents. I am hostile to multiculturalism not because I fear immigration, despise Muslims or want to reduce diversity but, on the contrary, because I favour immigration, oppose the growing hatred of

Muslims and welcome diversity. There is a long and important tradition of left-wing and progressive critiques of multiculturalism and of the ideas that underlie it, a tradition that has largely been buried by the right-wing assault in recent years. That assault has both reframed the debate about multiculturalism and made many on the Left reluctant to challenge it for fear of being associated with the likes of Bawer and Phillips, Wilders and Le Pen. This book is a critique of multiculturalism. It is also a critique of its critics. At its heart is the insistence that the challenge to multiculturalism and the challenge to its right-wing foes are inseparable.

Before we can discuss the claims both of multiculturalists and of their critics, we need first to unpack what we mean by 'multiculturalism'. Part of the problem is that the term has, in recent years, come to possess two meanings that are all too rarely distinguished. The first is what I call the lived experience of diversity. The second is multiculturalism as a political process the aim of which is to manage that diversity.

The experience of living in a society that is less insular, more vibrant and more cosmopolitan is something to welcome and celebrate. It is a case for cultural diversity, mass immigration, open borders and open minds. As a political process, however, multiculturalism means something different. It describes a set of policies, the aim of which is to manage and institutionalize diversity by putting people into ethnic and cultural boxes, defining individual needs and rights by virtue of the boxes into which people are put, and using those boxes to shape public policy. It is a case not for open borders and minds but for the policing of borders, whether physical, cultural or imaginative.

The conflation of lived experience and political policy has proved highly invidious. On the one hand, it has allowed many on the Right—and not just on the Right—to blame mass immigration for the failures of social policy and to turn minorities into the problem. On the other hand, it has forced many traditional liberals and radicals to abandon classical notions of liberty, such as an attachment to free speech, in the name of defending diversity.

The aim of *Multiculturalism and its Discontents* is to celebrate diversity while opposing multiculturalism. The book begins with a brief discussion of the historical and philosophical roots of multiculturalism, and of the philosophical debates surrounding it. It looks then at the political roots and social consequences of multicultural policy. Finally, I examine the contemporary critique of multiculturalism, to show that much of it is not simply wrong but also dangerous. The message of this book is that both multiculturalism and much of the discontent with it needs to be challenged.

2

Contemporary multiculturalism is a marriage between the Romantic idea of culture and an equally Romantic idea of identity. Romanticism is a concept that cultural historians find invaluable but almost impossible to define. It took many political forms—it lies at the root both of modern conservatism and many strands of radicalism—and appeared in different national versions. It was not a specific political or cultural view but, rather, described a cluster of attitudes and preferences: for the concrete over the abstract; the unique over the universal; nature over culture; the organic over the mechanical; emotion over reason; intuition over intellect; particular communities over abstract humanity.

These attitudes came to the fore towards the end of the eighteenth century largely in reaction to the predominant views of the Enlightenment. Much has been written about the varieties of beliefs and arguments within the eighteenth century and it is no longer fashionable to talk about *the* Enlightenment. Nevertheless, beneath the differences there were a number of beliefs that most of the

philosophes held in common and that distinguished Enlightenment thinkers from those
of both the seventeenth and the nineteenth
centuries. There was a broad consensus that
humans possessed a common nature; that
the same institutions and forms of governance would promote human flourishing in
all societies; that reason allowed humans to
discover these institutions; and that through
the development of such institutions social
inequalities and hierarchies could be mini-
mized and even erased.

The Romantic counter-Enlightenment
challenged all these beliefs. Enlightenment
philosophes saw progress as civilization over-
coming the resistance of traditional cultures with their peculiar superstitions, irra-
tional prejudices and outmoded institutions,
whereas the steamroller of progress and
modernity was precisely what the Romantics
feared. Enlightenment *philosophes* tended to
see civilization in the singular. Romantics
understood culture in the plural. Distinct

cultures were not aberrant forms to be destroyed but a precious inheritance to be cherished and protected.

The philosopher who perhaps best artic-ulated the Romantic notion of culture was the German Johann Gottfried Herder. He rejected the Enlightenment idea that reality was ordered in terms of universal, timeless, objective, unalterable laws that rational investigation could discover. He maintained, rather, that every activity, situation, historical period or civilization possessed a unique character. Scottish philosopher David Hume had suggested that 'Mankind are so much the same at all times and in all places that history informs us of nothing new or strange.'[4] Herder, on the contrary, insisted that history (and anthropology) reveals many things new and strange. Mankind was *not* the same at all times and in all places. What made each peo-ple or nation—or *volk*—unique was its *Kultur*: its particular language, literature, history and modes of living. The unique nature of each

volk was expressed through its *volksgeist*—
the unchanging spirit of a people refined
through history. Every culture was authentic
in its own terms, each adapted to its local
environment. The 'grand law of nature'
Herder proclaimed was 'let man be man. Let
him mould his condition according to what
he himself shall view as best.'[5]

Herder occupies an ambiguous role in
modern political thought. In the eighteenth
century, he saw himself as part of the Enlightenment tradition but also as someone forced
to challenge some of the basic precepts of
the *philosophes*—such as their stress on universal law and on the universal validity of
reason—in order to defend the cherished
ideals of equality. In the nineteenth century,
his concept of the *volksgeist* encouraged,
albeit unwittingly, the development of racial
science. *Volksgeist* became transformed into
racial make-up, an unchanging substance, the
foundation of all physical appearance and
mental potential and the basis for division and

difference within humankind. By the late nineteenth century, Herder's cultural pluralism came, paradoxically, also to give succour to the new anthropological notion of culture championed by critics of racial science. Franz Boas, the German American who played a key role in the development of cultural anthropology, sought, in the words of American historian George Stocking, to define the Romantic notion of 'the genius of the people' in terms other than those of racial heredity. His answer ultimately was the anthropological notion of culture. And in the twentieth century, Herder's relativism and particularism came to shape much of anti-racist thinking. The roots of barbarism, many came to believe, lay in Western arrogance, and the roots of Western arrogance lay in an unquestioning belief in the superiority of Enlightenment rationalism and universalism. The ambiguity of Herder's legacy still shapes contemporary multiculturalism. The Herderian idea of group differences gave rise to both racial and pluralist views and there remain, as we shall see, common bonds between racial and multicultural notions of human difference.

3

The second theme in Romantic thinking that is important to modern multiculturalism is the idea of identity. 'There is a certain way of being human that is *my* way,'[6] wrote Canadian philosopher Charles Taylor in his much discussed essay on 'The Politics of Recognition' (1994). 'I am called upon to live my life in this way. [. . .] Being true to myself means being true to my own originality.'[7] This sense of being 'true to myself' Taylor calls 'the ideal of "authenticity"'.[8] The ideal of the authentic self finds its origins in the Romantic notion of the 'inner voice' that spoke uniquely to every individual, guided their moral actions and expressed their true nature. The concept was developed in the 1950s by psychologists and sociologists, such as Erik Erikson and Alvin Gouldner, who pointed out that identity is not just a private matter but emerges in dialogue with others. Increasingly, identity came to be seen not as something that the self creates but as something through which the self is created. Identity is, in British sociologist Stuart Hall's words, 'formed and transformed continuously in relation to the ways in which we are represented or addressed in the cultural systems which surround us'.[9] The inner self, in other words, finds its home in the outer world by participating in a collective. But not just any collective. The world is composed of countless groups—philosophers, truck drivers, football supporters, drinkers, train-spotters, conservatives, communists and so on. But in contemporary debates about identity, each person's sense of who they truly are is seen as intimately linked primarily to a few special categories—collectives defined by gender, sexuality, religion, race and, in particular, culture. These comprise, of course, very different kinds of groups and the members of each are bound together by very different characteristics. Nevertheless, what collectives such as gender, sexuality, religion, race and culture have in common is that each is defined by a set of attributes that, whether rooted in biology, faith or history, is fixed in a certain sense and compels people to act in particular ways. Identity is that which is given, whether by nature, God or one's ancestors. 'I am called upon to live my life in this way,' as Taylor has put it. Unlike, say, politically defined collectives, these collectives are, in British philosopher John Gray's words, 'ascriptive, not elective [. . .] a matter of fate, not choice'.[10] The collectives that are important to the contemporary notion of identity are, in other words, the modern equivalents of Herder's *volks*. For individual identity to be authentic, collective identity must too. 'Just like individuals,' Taylor writes, 'a *Volk* should be true to itself, that is, its own culture.'[11]

The development of these views of culture and identity, rooted in the Romantic tradition (even if that rootedness remains often unrecognized, still less acknowledged), has transformed the way that many people have come to understand the relationship between equality and difference. For much of the past two centuries, important strands of liberal and radical thought drew upon Enlightenment insights to view equality as requiring the state to treat all citizens in the same fashion without regard to their race, religion or culture. Most contemporary multiculturalists, on the other hand, argue that people should be treated not equally despite their differences but differently because of them. There is, of course, a considerable diversity of views among multiculturalists; nonetheless, there are a number of common themes that underlie the arguments of most mainstream multiculturalists.

For most multiculturalists the heterogeneity and diversity that defines contemporary societies, especially in the West, makes old-style equality, rooted in Enlightenment notions of universalism, inadequate, even dangerous. The Enlightenment idea that all people flourish best under the same kinds of social institutions and forms of governance is a fantasy because the world is too complex and too varied to be subsumed under a single totalizing theory. Universalism is a 'Eurocentric' viewpoint, a means of imposing Euro-American ideas of rationality and objectivity on other peoples. In the place of universal rights come differential rights. 'Justice between groups,' as Canadian political philosopher Will Kymlicka, one of the most cogent contemporary advocates of multiculturalism, has put it, 'requires that members of different groups are accorded different rights.'[12]

An individual's cultural background frames their identity and helps define who they are. If we want to treat individuals with dignity and respect, we must also treat with dignity and respect the groups that furnish them with their sense of personal being. 'The liberal is in theory committed to equal respect for persons,' British philosopher Bhikhu Parekh has argued. 'Since human beings are culturally embedded, respect for them entails respect for their cultures and ways of life.'[13] British sociologist Tariq Modood takes this line of argument to make a distinction between what he calls the 'equality of individualism' and 'equality encompassing public ethnicity: equality as not having to hide or apologise for one's origins, family or community, but requiring others to show respect for them, and adapt public attitudes and arrangements so that the heritage they represent is encouraged rather than contemptuously expected to wither away'.[14] We cannot, in other words, treat individuals equally unless groups are also treated equally. And since, in the words of American scholar Iris Marion Young, 'groups cannot be socially equal unless their specific experience, culture and social contributions are publicly affirmed and recognized,'[15] so society must protect and nurture cultures, ensure their flourishing and, indeed, their survival. Some go further, requiring the state to ensure the survival of cultures not just in the present but in perpetuity. Taylor, for instance, suggests that the Canadian and Quebec governments should take steps to ensure the survival of the French language in Quebec 'through indefinite future generations'.[16]

Most multiculturalists would probably consider themselves as standing in the liberal Enlightenment tradition, if also highly critical of it. Yet, the rootedness of their argument in the Romantic counter-Enlightenment often gives a distinctly illiberal sheen to the policies they advocate. Take Modood's demand that people be *required* to give respect to various cultures and that public arrangements be adapted to accommodate them. Does this mean that schools should be forced to teach Creationism because it is part of Christian fundamentalist culture? Or should public arrangements be adapted to reflect the belief of many cultures that homosexuality is a sin? These are not simply abstract questions. Creationism, gay marriage, abortion, women's rights—these issues are at the heart of contemporary cultural conflicts.

'It is in the interest of every person to be fully integrated in a cultural group,'[17] Israeli sociologist Joseph Raz has written. This has become a common view in many multiculturalist claims. But what does it mean to be fully integrated? If a Muslim woman rejects sharia, is she demonstrating her lack of integration? What about a Jew who doesn't believe in the legitimacy of the Jewish state? Or a French Quebecois who speaks only English? Would Galileo have challenged the authority of the Church if he had been 'fully integrated' into his culture? Or Thomas Paine have supported the French Revolution? Or Salman Rushdie written *The Satanic Verses* (1988)?

Part of the problem here is a slippage between the idea of humans as culture-bearing creatures and the idea that humans have to bear a *particular* culture. Clearly, no human can live outside culture. But then no human does. To say that no human can live outside culture is not to say, however, that they have to live inside a *particular* one. To view humans as culture-bearing is to view them as social beings and hence as transformative beings. It suggests that they have the capacity for change, for progress and for the creation of universal moral and political forms through reason and dialogue. To view humans as having to bear specific cultures is, on the contrary, to deny such a capacity for transformation. It suggests that every human being is so shaped by a particular culture that to change or undermine that culture would be to undermine the very dignity of that individual. It suggests that the biological fact of, say, Jewish or Bangladeshi ancestry somehow makes a human being incapable of living well except as a participant of Jewish or Bangladeshi culture. This would only make sense if Jews or Bangladeshis were biologically distinct—in other words if cultural identity was really about racial difference.

The relationship between cultural identity and racial difference becomes even clearer if we look at the argument made by many multiculturalists that minority cultures under threat must be protected and preserved. If a 'culture is decaying,' Israeli sociologists Avishai Margalit and Joseph Raz argue, then 'the options and opportunities open to its members will shrink, become less attractive, and their pursuit less likely to be successful.'[18] So society must step in to prevent such decay. Kymlicka similarly argues that since cultures are essential to peoples' lives, where 'the survival of a culture is not guaranteed, and where it is threatened with debasement or decay, we must act to protect it.'[19] For Taylor, once 'we're concerned with identity', nothing 'is more legitimate than one's aspiration that it never be lost'.[20] Hence a culture needs to be protected not just in the here and now but through 'indefinite future generations'.

A century ago, intellectuals worried about the 'degeneration of the race'. Today we fear cultural decay. Is the notion of cultural decay any more coherent than that of racial degeneration? Cultures certainly change and develop—a point few multiculturalists would dispute. But what does it mean for a culture to decay? Or for an identity to be lost? Kymlicka draws a distinction between the 'existence of a culture' and 'its "character" at any given moment'.[21] The character can change but such changes are only acceptable if the existence of that culture is not threatened. But how can a culture exist if that existence is not embodied in its character?

By 'character' Kymlicka seems to mean the actuality of a culture: what people do, how they live their lives, the rules and regulations and institutions that frame their existence. So, in making the distinction between character and existence, he seems to be suggesting that Jewish, Navajo or French culture is not defined by what Jewish, Navajo or French people are actually doing. For, if Jewish culture is simply that which Jewish people do or French culture is simply that which French people do, then cultures could never decay or perish—they would always exist in the activities of people.

If a culture is not defined by what its members are doing, then by what is it defined? The only answer can be that it is defined by what its members *should* be doing. African American writer Richard Wright described one of his finest creations, Bigger Thomas, the hero of his 1940 novel *Native Son*, as a man 'bereft of a culture'.[22] The Negro, Wright argued, 'possessed a rich and complex culture when he was brought to these alien shores'.[23] But that culture was 'taken from him'. Bigger Thomas' ancestors had been enslaved. In the process of enslavement, they had been torn from their ancestral homes and forcibly deprived of the practices and institutions that they understood as their culture. Hence Bigger Thomas, and every black American, behaved very differently from his ancestors.

Slavery was an abomination and clearly had a catastrophic impact on black Americans. But however inhuman the treatment of slaves, and however deep its impact on black American life, why should it amount to a descendant of slaves being 'bereft of a culture'? This can only be if we believe that Bigger Thomas *should* be behaving in certain ways that he isn't, in ways that his ancestors used to behave. In other words, if we believe that what you should be doing is defined by the fact that your ancestors were doing it. Culture here has become defined by biological descent. And biological descent is a polite way of saying 'race'. As American literary critic Walter Benn Michaels puts it, 'In order for a culture to be lost [. . .] it must be separable from one's actual behaviour, and in order for it to be separable from one's actual behaviour it must be anchorable in race.'[24]

The logic of the preservationist arguments is that every culture has a pristine form, its original state. It decays when it is no longer in that form. There are echoes here of the concept of 'type' that was at the heart of nineteenth-century racial science. A racial type was a group of human beings linked by a set of fundamental characteristics unique to it. Each type was separated from others by a sharp discontinuity; there was rarely any doubt as to which type an individual belonged. Each type remained constant through time. There were severe limits to how much any member of a type could drift away from the fundamental ground plan by which the type was constituted. These are also the characteristics that constitute a culture in much of today's multiculturalism talk. For all the talk about culture as fluid and changing, multiculturalism invariably leads people to think of human cultures in fixed terms. Indeed, it is difficult to imagine how multicultural policy could conceive of cultures in any other way. How could rights be accorded to cultures or cultures be recognized or preserved if they did not possess rigid boundaries?

4

The irony in the contemporary obsession with cultural differences is that we have all become multiculturalists at the very time the world is becoming less, not more, plural. 'When I was a child,' the Ghanaian-born American philosopher Kwame Anthony Appiah recalls, 'we lived in a household where you could hear at least three mother tongues spoken every day. Ghana, with a population close to that of New York State, has several dozen languages in active use and no one language that is spoken at home—or even fluently understood—by a majority of the population.' So why is it, he asks, that in the US 'which seems so much less diverse than most other societies we are so preoccupied with diversity and inclined to conceive of it as cultural?'[25]

The proportion of foreign-born Americans is far less than it was at the beginning of the twentieth century. Intermarriage between immigrant groups continues to increase. More than 97 per cent of Americans speak English. Even among Hispanics, the one ethnic group defined by language, the proportion of non-English speakers is a quarter of what it was among all immigrants at the beginning of the twentieth century. Then new immigrants did not simply speak their own language but read their own newspapers, ate their own food and lived their own lives. In 1923, for instance, the Polish community alone published 67 weekly newspapers, 18 monthlies and 19 dailies, the largest of which had a circulation of more than 100,000.[26]

Today, not just language but also the shopping mall, the sports field, the Hollywood film and the TV sitcom all serve to bind differences and create a set of experiences and cultural practices that is more common than at any time in the past. Indeed, even before today's immigrants set foot on US soil, they are probably more American than previous generations of Americans. Even immigrants from non-European countries are, as American sociologist Dennis Wrong suggests, 'probably less unfamiliar with the major features of the society than were, say, South Italian or Slavic peasants in the late-nineteenth or early-twentieth centuries'.[27]

Much the same is true of Europe. There has been considerable debate in recent years about the impact of mass migration, in particular, of Muslims, and on social cohesion and national identity, a debate I shall explore more closely later. At the heart of this debate lies the belief, held by both sides, that European nations used to be homogeneous but have become diverse. It is a claim that does not stand up to scrutiny. Both sides are suffering from a collective memory loss.

At the time of the French Revolution, for instance, less than half the population of France spoke French and only 12 per cent spoke it 'correctly'. American historian Eugene Weber has shown the extraordinary modernizing effort that was required in the nineteenth century to unify France and its rural populations, and the traumatic and lengthy process of cultural, educational, political and economic 'self-colonization' that this entailed. These developments created the modern French nation and allowed for notions of French (and European) superiority over non-European cultures. It also reinforced a sense of how socially and anthropologically alien was the mass of the rural, and indeed urban, population. In an address to the Medico-Psychological Society of Paris in 1857, the Christian socialist Philippe Buchez considered the meaning of social differentiation within France:

> Consider a population like ours, placed in the most favourable

circumstances; possessed of a powerful civilization; amongst the highest ranking nations in science, the arts and industry. Our task now, I maintain, is to find out how it can happen that within a population such as ours, races may form—not merely one but several races—so miserable, inferior and bastardized that they may be classed below the most inferior savage races, for their inferiority is sometimes beyond cure.[28]

Victorian England, too, viewed the urban working class and the rural poor as the racial Other. A vignette of working class life in the *Saturday Review*, a widely read liberal magazine of the era, is typical of English middle-class attitudes of this era:

The Bethnal Green poor [. . .] are a caste apart, a race of whom we know nothing, whose lives are of quite different complexion from ours, persons with whom we have no point of contact. And although there is not yet quite the same separation of classes or castes in the country, yet the great mass of the agricultural poor are divided from the educated and the comfortable, from squires and parsons and tradesmen, by a barrier which custom has forged through long centuries, and which only very exceptional circumstances ever beat down, and then only for an instant. The slaves are separated from the whites by more glaring [. . .] marks of distinction; but still distinctions and separations, like those of English classes which always endure, which last from the cradle to the grave, which prevent anything like association or companionship, produce a general effect on the life of the extreme poor, and subject them to isolation, which offer a very fair parallel to the separation of the slaves from the whites.[29]

Modern Bethnal Green is not home to warehousemen or costermongers but lies at the heart of the Bangladeshi community in East London. Today's 'Bethnal Green poor' are often seen as culturally and racially distinct. But only those on the fringes of politics would compare the distinctiveness of Bangladeshis to that of slaves. The sense of apartness was far greater in Victorian England than it is in contemporary Britain. And that is because, in reality, the social and cultural differences between a Victorian gentleman or factory owner on the one hand and a farmhand or a machinist on the other were much greater than they are between a white resident and one of Bangladeshi origin living in Bethnal Green today.

However much they may view each other as different, a 16-year-old of Bangladeshi origin living in Bethnal Green, or a 16-year-old of Algerian origin living in Marseilles, or a 16-year-old of Turkish origin living in Berlin, probably wears the same clothes, listens to the same music, watches the same TV shows, follows the same football club as a 16-year-old white child in that same city. A 60-something white Briton would probably find a 20-something white Briton more culturally alien than either would an Asian or African Caribbean of their own generation.

There is, then, nothing new in plural societies. From a historical perspective, contemporary societies, even those transformed by mass immigration, are not particularly plural. What is different today is the *perception* that we are living in a uniquely plural world, and the perception of such pluralism in largely cultural terms. The debate about multiculturalism is one in which certain differences (culture, ethnicity, faith) have come to be regarded as important while others (such as class, say, or generation), which used to be perceived as important in the past, have come to be seen as less relevant. Why this has happened I will return to later.

5

The idea that European nations used to be homogenous but have become plural is one myth accepted by both sides in the multiculturalism debate. Another is that such nations have become multicultural because minorities wished to assert their differences. The question of the cultural difference of immigrants has certainly preoccupied political elites. It is not a question, however, that, until recently, has particularly engaged immigrants themselves.

Take the UK. The arrival of large numbers of immigrants from India, Pakistan and the Caribbean in the late 1940s and 50s led to considerable unease about its impact on traditional concepts of Britishness. As a Colonial Office report of 1953 observed, 'a large coloured community as a noticeable feature of our social life would weaken [. . .] the concept of England or Britain to which people of British stock throughout the Commonwealth are attached.'[30]

The migrants certainly brought with them a host of traditions and habits and cultural mores from their homelands, of which they were often proud. But they were rarely concerned with preserving cultural differences and did not think of it as a political issue. What inspired them was the struggle not for cultural identity but for political equality. They recognized that at the heart of that struggle was the creation of a commonality of values, hopes and aspirations between migrants and indigenous Britons, not an articulation of unbridgeable differences.

This is equally true of the group whose traditions, beliefs and mores are widely perceived to be most distinct from those of Western societies, and hence the group that is supposedly most demanding that its differences be publicly recognized: Muslims.

The patterns of Muslim migration have, in fact, been little different from that of many other communities. The best way to understand it is in terms of three generations:

the first generation that came to Europe in the 1950s and 60s; the second generation that was born or grew up in the 1970s and 80s; and the third generation that has come of age since then. This is, I know, a somewhat crude characterization, but it is useful to have a broad-brush understanding of the changing relationships between migrants and European societies. My examples are primarily from the UK but the structure applies also to immigration to other European countries.

The first generation of Muslim immigrants to the UK, who came almost entirely from the Indian subcontinent, were pious in their faith but wore it lightly. British writer and theatre director Pervaiz Khan, whose family came to the UK in the 1950s, remembers his father and uncles going to the pub for a pint. 'They did not bring drink home,' he says, 'and they did not make a song and dance about it. But everyone knew they drank. And they were never ostracized for it.' No woman wore a hijab, let alone a niqab or burqa. His family 'rarely fasted at Ramadan,' Khan says, 'and often missed Friday prayers. They did not boast about it. But they were not pariahs for it. It is very different from today.'[31]

Khan's experience was not unusual. My parents were similar, as were those of most of my friends. Their faith expressed for them a relationship with God, not a sacrosanct public identity. Islam was not, in their eyes, an all-encompassing philosophy.

The second generation—my generation—was primarily secular. It did not think of itself as Muslim or Hindu or Sikh, or even often as Asian but, rather, as black. Black was for us not an ethnic label but a political badge. The 'Muslim community', in the sense of a community that defined itself solely, or even primarily, by faith, did not exist in the 1970s. Neither did the Sikh community, nor the Hindu community.

Unlike our parents' generation, which had largely put up with discrimination, we were fierce in our opposition to racism. We were equally fierce in our opposition to religion and to the traditions that often marked immigrant communities. Religious organizations were, in my youth, barely visible. The organizations that bound together migrant communities were secular, often socialist: the Asian Youth Movements, for instance, or the Indian Workers Association.

It is only with the generation that has come of age since the late-1980s that the question of cultural differences has come to be seen as important. A generation that, ironically, is far more integrated and 'Westernized' than the first generation is also the one that is most insistent on maintaining its 'difference'. That in itself should make us question the received wisdom about how and why multicultural policies emerged.

The shift in the meaning of a single word expresses this transformation. When I was growing up, to be 'radical' was to be militantly secular, self-consciously Western and avowedly left-wing: to be someone like me.

Today, 'radical' in a Muslim context means
the very opposite. It describes a religious fundamentalist, someone who is anti-Western,
who is opposed to secularism.

What is true of the UK is true also of
many other European countries. The irony
in France, for instance, is that for all the cur-
rent hostility of the French state to Islam and
to public displays of Islamic identity such as
the burqa, for most of the post-war years,
while migrant workers were defiantly secular,
successive governments regarded such secularism a threat and attempted to foist religion upon them, encouraging them to
maintain their traditional cultural identities.

Paul Dijoud, minister for immigrant
workers in the 1970s government of Valéry
Giscard d'Estaing, declared that 'The right to
a cultural identity allows the immigrant,
despite his geographical distance, to stay close
to his country.'[32] The government sought in
Islam 'a stabilizing force which would turn
the faithful from deviance, delinquency or

membership of unions or revolutionary parties'.[33] When a series of strikes hit car factories in the late 1970s, the government encouraged employers to build prayer rooms in an effort to wean immigrant workers, who formed a large proportion of the workforce, away from militant activity.

The claim that minority communities have demanded that their cultural differences be publicly recognized and affirmed is, then, historically false. That demand has emerged only recently. The myth that multiculturalism was a response to minority demands gets cause and effect the wrong way round. Minority communities did not force politicians to introduce multicultural policies. Rather, the desire to celebrate one's cultural identity has itself, in part at least, been shaped by the implementation of multicultural policies.

6

Over the past two decades, many European nations have adopted multicultural policies or at least promoted a multicultural approach, but they have done so in distinct ways. The UK and Norway, Sweden and Germany, the Netherlands and Denmark: every country has its own specific multicultural history to tell. I want to look at two contrasting histories, that of the UK and of Germany, to understand what they have in common despite their differences and what these commonalities tell us about multiculturalism itself.

The arrival of large number of immigrants in the UK in the 1950s created conflicting pressures on policy-makers. While they welcomed the influx of new labour, there was considerable unease about the impact that such immigration might have on traditional concepts of Britishness.

But even in the 1950s, it was clear that old-fashioned notions of Britishness could not be sustained for long. For a start, it was a form of national identity rooted in a Britain and an empire that was already crumbling. Moreover, the experience of Nazism and the Holocaust had rendered virtually unusable the kind of racial exclusiveness embodied in this notion of national identity. In any case, by the end of the 1950s, black immigrants were already a fact of life in the UK. Despite the continued attempts over the next few decades by politicians from Enoch Powell to Margaret Thatcher to formulate a racially exclusive concept of Britishness, it was already apparent by the 1960s that British identity would have to be reformulated to include the presence in this country of black citizens.

Policy-makers embarked, therefore, on a new twin-track strategy in response to immigration. On the one hand, they imposed increasingly restrictive immigration controls specifically designed to exclude non-white immigrants. On the other, they instituted a framework of legislation aimed at outlawing racial discrimination and at facilitating the integration of black and Asian communities into British society.

The twin-track strategy helped promote the idea of the UK as a tolerant, pluralistic nation that was determined to stamp out any trace of discriminatory practice based on racial or ethnic difference. In the words of Roy Jenkins, Labour home secretary in the mid-1960s, the UK set out to create 'cultural diversity, coupled with equal opportunity, in an atmosphere of mutual tolerance'.[34] At the same time, though, the linking of immigration and integration implied that social problems arose from the very presence in the UK of culturally distinct immigrants. As the (liberal) Tory shadow home secretary Reginald Maudling put it in a parliamentary debate in 1968, 'The problem arises quite simply from the arrival in this country of many people of wholly alien cultures, habits and outlooks.'[35] From the beginning, then, the problem of race relations was viewed not so much as one of racial discrimination but, rather, of cultural differences and of the inability of black immigrants to be sufficiently British.

Immigrants, too, were concerned with the question of difference, but in a different way. What preoccupied them was not the desire to be treated differently but the fact that they *were* treated differently. Throughout the 1960s and 70s, four big issues dominated the struggle for political equality: opposition to discriminatory immigration controls; the struggle against workplace discrimination; the fight against racist attacks; and, most explosively, the issue of police brutality. These issues, individually and collectively, embodied the demand not for cultural identity but for political equality. They politicized a new generation of black and Asian activists and came to a fiery climax in the riots that tore through the UK's inner cities in the late 1970s and early 1980s.

On the afternoon of Friday, 10 April 1981, police in Brixton, south London, stopped Michael Bailey, a 19-year-old black man bleeding from a knife wound. Witnesses alleged that he was bundled into a police car and that no ambulance was called. A crowd gathered, surrounded the car and eventually freed Bailey. Soon there were running battles with the police. The arrest the following day of another black man sparked off a full-scale riot. That evening, the first petrol bombs were thrown. Shocked viewers watched on the TV news that night scenes they had previously witnessed on the streets of Belfast or Derry. By the following day, 30 buildings had burnt down and another 120 had been damaged. More than 100 cars and vans, including 56 police vehicles, were torched. Three hundred policemen and 65 civilians were seriously injured. Up to 5,000 people were said to be involved in the riot.

The Brixton riot came to symbolize the breakdown of race relations in the UK. It was the first in a series of violent eruptions that rippled out through the rest of London and well beyond. From Brixton the violence touched Peckham, Southall, Wood Green, Finsbury Park, Woolwich, Forest Gate and Notting Hill in London. It reached into Liverpool, Birkenhead, Sheffield, Manchester, Hull, Newcastle and Preston in the north of England. It sparked off riots in the Midlands towns of Coventry, Birmingham, Leicester, Derby and Nottingham. Towns in the south of England rarely thought of as racial tinderboxes caught alight too: Southampton, Cirencester, High Wycombe, Gloucester, Luton, Reading and Aldershot. In Wales, rioting broke out in Cardiff. Finally, the violence returned to Brixton in July 1981. 'Measured by any standards,' the black activist Darcus Howe has written, 'this revolt assumed serious insurrectionary proportions.'[36]

The authorities recognized that unless minority communities were given a political stake in the system, their frustration could threaten the stability of UK cities. It was against this background that the policies of multiculturalism emerged. The then ruling Conservative government, led by Margaret Thatcher, wanted to reach out to immigrant communities but was ill-placed to do so, for few within black and Asian communities were willing to place their trust in what they regarded as the party of racism. Labour-controlled local authorities possessed the moral currency to help rebuild the inner cities, physically and socially. They pioneered a new strategy of making black and Asian communities feel part of British society by organizing consultations, drawing up equal-opportunity policies, establishing race-relations units and dispensing millions of pounds in grants to minority organizations. At the heart of the strategy was a redefinition of racism. Racism now meant not simply the denial of equal rights but also the denial of the right to be different. The old idea of British values or a British identity was, the new municipal anti-racists argued, defunct. Rather than be expected to accept British values, or to adopt a British identity, different peoples should have the right to express their identities, explore their own histories, formulate their own values, pursue their own lifestyles.

Scepticism about the idea of a common national identity arose in part from cynicism about the idea of 'Britishness'. There was widespread recognition among blacks and Asians that talk about Britishness was a means not of extending citizenship to all Britons, whatever their colour and creed, but of denying equal rights to certain groups. 'British' for many meant 'white'. But the new anti-racist strategy did not simply challenge old-fashioned ideas of Britishness. It transformed the very meaning of equality. Equality now meant not possessing the same rights as everyone else, despite differences of race, ethnicity, culture or faith, but possessing different rights, because of them.

In 2000, the Commission on the Future of Multi-Ethnic Britain, chaired by Bhikhu Parekh, published its report that famously concluded that Britain was a 'community of communities' in which equality 'must be defined in a culturally sensitive way and applied in a discriminating but not discriminatory manner'.[37] The Parekh report has come to be seen as defining the essence of multiculturalism. But the arguments at its heart had emerged out of the response of the authorities, two decades earlier, to the inner city riots and to the fierce anger about racism. The consequences of these arguments and of these policies I shall discuss later. But first, I want to turn to the question of multiculturalism in Germany.

7

Germany's road to multiculturalism was different from Britain's, though the starting point was the same. Like many West European nations, Germany faced an immense labour shortage in the post-war years and actively recruited foreign workers. Unlike in Britain, the new workers came not from former colonies but initially from Italy, Spain and Greece and then from Turkey. And they came not as immigrants, still less as potential citizens, but as *Gastarbeiter* or 'guest workers', who were expected to return to their country of origin when no longer required to service the German economy.

Over time, however, immigrants became transformed from a temporary necessity to a permanent presence. This was partly because Germany continued to rely on their labour and partly because immigrants, and more so their children, came to see Germany as home. But the German state continued to view them as outsiders and to refuse them citizenship.

Citizenship in Germany was, until recently, based on the principle of *jus sanguinis*, by which one could only acquire citizenship if one's parents were also citizens. It was a principle that excluded from citizenship not just first-generation immigrants but also their German-born children. A new nationality law passed in 1999 makes it easier for immigrants to acquire citizenship. Nevertheless, most Turks remain outsiders. There are nearly four million people of Turkish origin in Germany today. Barely half a million have managed to acquire citizenship.

Instead of creating an open society, into which immigrants were welcome as equals, German politicians from the 1980s onwards dealt with the so-called Turkish problem through a policy of multiculturalism. In place of citizenship and a genuine status in society, immigrants were 'allowed' to keep their own culture, language and lifestyle. The consequence was the creation of parallel communities (a phrase that came to be popularized in the official report into the 2001 riots in Oldham, in northern England). The policy did not so much represent respect for diversity as provide a means of avoiding the issue of how to create a common, inclusive culture.

First-generation immigrants were broadly secular and those that were religious wore their faith lightly. Today, almost one-third of adult Turks in Germany regularly attend mosque, a higher rate than among Turkish communities elsewhere in Western Europe, and higher even than in many parts of Turkey. First-generation women almost never wore headscarves. Many of their daughters do. Without any incentive to participate in the national community, many did not bother learning German.

At the same time as Germany's multicultural policies encouraged immigrants to be at best indifferent to mainstream German society, at worst openly hostile to it, they also made Germans increasingly antagonistic towards Turks. The sense of what it meant to be German was in part defined against the values and beliefs of the excluded immigrant communities. And having excluded them, it has become easier to scapegoat immigrants for Germany's social ills. A 2010 poll showed that more than one-third of Germans thought that the country is 'over-run by foreigners' and more than half felt that Arabs were 'unpleasant'.[38]

In Germany, the formal denial of citizenship to immigrants led to the policy of multiculturalism. In the UK, the promotion of multicultural policies led to the de facto treatment of individuals from minority communities not as citizens but simply as members of particular ethnic groups. The consequence in both cases has been the creation of fragmented societies, the alienation of many minority groups and the scapegoating of immigrants.

8

The story I have told so far is of a Europe that is not as plural as many imagine it to be, and of immigrants less assertive of their cultural identities than they are claimed to be. Multicultural policies emerged not because migrants demanded them but primarily because the political elite needed them to manage immigration and to assuage anger created by racism.

Why, then, have we come to imagine that we are living in a particularly plural society, in which our cultural identities are all-important? The answer lies in a complex set of social, political and economic changes over the past half century, changes that include the narrowing of the political sphere, the collapse of the Left, the demise of class politics and the erosion of more universalist visions of social change. Many of these changes helped pave the way for multicultural policies. At the same time, the implementation of such policies helped create a more fragmented society. Or, to put it another way, multicultural policies have entrenched, and in many cases created, the very problems they were meant to have resolved. I want to demonstrate this through two examples. The first is a riot in Britain, which is now barely remembered, the second a cartoon crisis in Denmark, about which almost everyone knows.

In 1985, the Handsworth area of Birmingham, UK, was rocked by riots. Blacks, Asians and whites took to the streets in protest against poverty, unemployment and, in particular, police harassment. In the violence that followed, two people were killed and dozens injured. It was almost the last flicker of the 1980s inner city conflagrations.

Twenty years later, in October 2005, another riot erupted in the the neighbouring area of Lozells. This time the fighting was not between youth and police but between blacks and Asians. An unsubstantiated—and almost certainly untrue—rumour that a Jamaican girl had been raped by a group of Asian men led to a weekend of violence between the two communities during which a young black man was murdered.

Why did two communities that had fought side by side in 1985 fight against each other 20 years later? The answer lies largely in the policies introduced by the Birmingham Council after the original riots. In response to those riots, the council proposed a new political framework for the engagement of minority communities. It created nine so-called umbrella groups, organizations based on ethnicity and faith that were supposed to represent the needs of their particular communities while aiding policy development and resource allocation. These included the African and Caribbean People's Movement, the Bangladeshi Islamic Projects Consultative Committee, the Birmingham Chinese Society, the Council of Black-Led Churches, the Hindu Council, the Irish Forum, the Vietnamese Association, the Pakistani Forum and the Sikh Council of Gurdwaras.

Birmingham Council's policies were aimed at drawing minority communities into the democratic process. The trouble was that there was precious little democracy in the process. The groups themselves had no democratic mandate, indeed no mandate at all. After all why should the Council of Black-Led Churches presume to speak for the needs and aspirations of African Caribbeans in Birmingham? Why should all Bangladeshis be represented by an Islamic organization or all Sikhs by the gurdwaras? And, indeed, what is *the* Bangladeshi community or *the* Sikh community and what are its needs and aspirations? Imagine if the council had set up a 'White Forum' to represent the needs of the white community in Birmingham. Could such a group have represented the interests of all white people in Birmingham? Clearly not. Why should we imagine that Bangladeshis or Sikhs or African Caribbeans are any different?

This points up a paradox in the multicultural vision. The starting point of multicultural policies is the acceptance of societies as diverse. Yet, there is an unstated assumption that such diversity ends at the edges of minority communities. Birmingham Council's policies, like much multicultural policy, treated minority communities as homogeneous wholes, ignoring conflicts within those communities. As one council report put it:

'The perceived notion of the homogeneity of minority ethnic communities has informed a great deal of race equality work to date. The effect of this, amongst others, has been to place an over-reliance on individuals who are seen to represent the needs or views of the whole community and resulted in simplistic approaches toward tackling community needs.'[39]

Multicultural policies, in other words, have not responded to the needs of communities but, to a large degree, have helped *create* those communities by imposing identities on people and by ignoring internal conflicts arising out of class, gender and intra-religious differences. They have empowered not minority communities but so-called community leaders who owe their position and influence largely to the relationship they possesse with the state.

At the same time as they ignored conflicts within minority communities, Birmingham's policies created conflicts between them. As one academic study of these policies observes: 'The model of engagement through Umbrella Groups tended to result in competition between BME [black and minority ethnic] communities for resources. Rather than prioritizing needs and cross-community working, the different Umbrella Groups generally attempted to maximize their own interests.'[40]

Once political power and financial resources became allocated by ethnicity, then people began to identify themselves only in terms of those ethnicities, and only those ethnicities. 'People are forced into a very one-dimensional view of themselves by the way that equality policies work,' observes Joy Warmington of the Birmingham Race Action Partnership, a council-funded but independent equalities organization.[41] People mobilize on the basis of how they feel they will get the resources to tackle the issues important to them. And in Birmingham, it helps to say that you are campaigning for the needs of your ethnic or religious community because policies have tended to emphasize ethnicity as a key to entitlement. It has become accepted as good practice to allocate resources on ethnic or religious lines. Rather than thinking of meeting people's needs or about distributing resources more equitably, organizations are forced to think about the distribution of ethnicity. And people begin to think in those terms too.

Imagine that you are a secular Bangladeshi living in a run-down area of Birmingham. You don't think of yourself as a Muslim, you may not even think of yourself as Bangladeshi. But you want a new community centre in your area. It is difficult to get the council's attention by insisting that your area is poor or disadvantaged. But if you were to say that the Muslim community is deprived or lacking, then council coffers suddenly open up, not because the council is particularly inclined to help Muslims but because being Muslim, unlike being 'poor' or 'disadvantaged', registers in the bureaucratic mind as an authentic identity. Over time, you come to see yourself in those terms, not just because those identities provide you with access to power, influence and resources, but also because those identities possess a social reality through receiving constant confirmation and affirmation. It is how you are seen; so, it is how you come to see yourself. You come to fear and resent African Caribbeans and Sikhs and the Irish, partly because they are competitors for that pot of council largesse and power, and partly because the rules of the game are that your identity has to be affirmed as distinctive and different from the identities of other groups. Being Muslim also means being not-Irish, not-Sikh and not–African Caribbean.

The consequence is what the Nobel Prize–winning Indian economist Amartya Sen has called 'plural monoculturalism'[42]—policy driven by the myth that society is made up of a series of distinct, homogeneous cultures that dance round each other. The policy, ironically, has helped make such a segmented society a reality. The result in Birmingham was to entrench divisions between black and Asian communities to an extent that it sparked inter-communal rioting.

9

Not only have multicultural policies entrenched, with disastrous consequences, the idea of homogeneous communities, they have also enabled the most conservative and reactionary figures to be seen as the authentic voices of those communities. Consider, for instance, the controversy over the Danish cartoons. We all know what happened. A Danish newspaper, *Jyllands-Posten*, published a series of inflammatory cartoons depicting Prophet Muhammad. Islam forbids the depiction of the Prophet. So millions of Muslims worldwide were enraged to the point of violence.

Except that it never happened like that. For a start, there is no universal Islamic prohibition on the representation of the

Prophet. Rather, it was common to portray him until comparatively recently. The prohibition against such depictions only emerged in the seventeenth century. Even over the past 400 years, a number of Islamic, especially Shi'ite, traditions have accepted the pictorial representation of the Prophet. Edinburgh University Library in Scotland, the Bibliothèque Nationale in Paris, the Metropolitan Museum of Art in New York and the Topkapi Palace Museum in Istanbul, all contain dozens of Persian, Ottoman and Afghan manuscripts depicting him. His face can be seen in many mosques too—even in Iran. A seventeenth-century mural in the Iman Zahdah Chah Zaid Mosque in the Iranian town of Isfahan, for instance, shows a Muhammad whose facial features are clearly visible.

Even today, few Muslims have a problem with seeing the Prophet's face. Shortly after *Jyllands-Posten* published the cartoons, the Egyptian newspaper *Al Fagr* reprinted them. They were accompanied by a critical commentary, but *Al Fagr* did not think it necessary to blank out Muhammad's face and faced no opprobrium for not doing so. Egypt's religious and political authorities, even as they were demanding an apology from the Danish prime minister, raised no objections to *Al Fagr*'s full-frontal photos.

So, if there is no universal prohibition on the depiction of Muhammad, why were Muslims universally appalled by the caricatures? They weren't; and those that were, were driven as much by political zeal as by theological fervour.

The publication of the cartoons in September 2005 caused no immediate reaction, even in Denmark. Journalists, disappointed by the lack of controversy, contacted a number of imams for their response. Among the first was Ahmed Abu Laban. He seized upon the cartoons to transform himself into a spokesman for Denmark's Muslims, demanding an apology not just from the newspaper but from the Danish prime minister, too, and organizing a demonstration outside the offices of *Jyllands-Posten*. Yet, however hard the imams pushed, they could not provoke major outrage either in Denmark or abroad. At the beginning of December 2005, a group of Danish imams compiled a 40-page dossier about the cartoons to circulate to delegates at a summit of the Organization of the Islamic Conference (OIC) in Mecca. Two weeks later, a second delegation of Danish imams toured various Middle Eastern, Near Eastern and North African countries. At the end of January, Saudi Arabia recalled its ambassador from Denmark and launched a consumer boycott of Danish goods. In response, a swathe of European newspapers republished the cartoons in 'solidarity' with *Jyllands-Posten*. It was only now—more than four months after the cartoons had been originally published, more than four months of strenuous effort to create a controversy—that the issue became more than a minor diplomatic kerfuffle, with protests in India, Pakistan, Indonesia, Egypt,

Afghanistan, Libya, Syria, Iran, Nigeria, Palestine and elsewhere, Danish embassies torched in Beirut, Damascus and Tehran, and more than 250 people losing their lives in the violence.

Why did journalists contact Abu Laban in the first place? His Islamic Society of Denmark had little support. Out of a population of 180,000 Danish Muslims, fewer than 1,000 attended the society's Friday prayers. He was, however, infamous for his support for Osama bin Laden (whom he called a businessman and freedom fighter) and for the 9/11 attack ('I mourn dry tears for the victims' was Laban's reported response). From a journalistic viewpoint it made sense to get a quote from someone so controversial. But politically, too, it made sense.

Western liberals have come to see figures like Abu Laban as the true, authentic voice of Islam. The Danish MP Nasser Khader, who is Muslim though not religious, tells of a conversation with Toger Seidenfaden, editor of

Politiken, a left-wing newspaper highly critical of the caricatures. 'He said to me that cartoons insulted all Muslims,' Khader recalls. 'I said I was not insulted. He said, "But you're not a real Muslim".'[43] In liberal eyes, in other words, to be a real Muslim is to find the cartoons offensive. Once Muslim authenticity is so defined, then only a figure such as Abu Laban can be seen as a true Muslim voice. As the Danish sociologist Jytte Klausen, author of *The Cartoons that Shook the World* (2009), the definitive account of the affair, has observed, the Danish cartoons, 'have become not just a tool for extremism but also created a soap opera in the West about what Muslims "do" with respect to pictures'.[44] Or, as Khader has put it, 'What I find really offensive is that journalists and politicians see the fundamentalists as the real Muslims.'[45] The myths about the Danish cartoons—that all Muslims hated the cartoons and that it was a theological conflict—helped turn Abu Laban into an authentic voice of Islam and to silence other voices. At the same time, Abu Laban's views seemed to confirm the myths about the Danish cartoons.

The question at the heart of the Danish controversy is not simply 'what is offensive?' but also 'who decides what is offensive?' In other words: 'Who speaks for the community?—Abu Laban or Nasser Khader?' That is also the question at the heart of many of the flashpoints about 'offensiveness', from the global confrontation over Rushdie's *Satanic Verses* to the local struggle over Sikh playwright Gurpreet Kaur Bhatti's play *Behzti*, which was forced off stage in 2005 by Sikh activists in Birmingham who objected to it.

10

The issue of free speech and the giving of offence have become central to the multiculturalism debate. Speech, many argue, must necessarily be less free in a plural society. For such societies to function and be fair, we need to show respect for all cultures and beliefs. And to do so requires us to police pubic discourse about those cultures and beliefs, both to minimize friction between antagonistic cultures and beliefs, and to protect the dignity of individuals embedded in them. As Modood puts it, 'If people are to occupy the same political space without conflict, they mutually have to limit the extent to which they subject each others' fundamental beliefs to criticism.'[46] One of the ironies of living in a plural society, it seems, is that the preservation of diversity requires us to leave *less* room for a diversity of views.

The problem with this line of argument is that what is often regarded as offence *to* a community is in reality a debate *within* that community. That is why so many of the flashpoints over offensiveness have been over works produced by minority artists—from Salman Rushdie to Gurpreet Kaur Bhatti, from Hanif Kureishi to Sooreh Hera, from Taslima Nasrin to Maqbool Fida Husain.

Consider the controversy over *The Satanic Verses*. Neither Rushdie nor his critics spoke for the Muslim community. Each represented different strands of opinion. Rushdie gave voice to a radical, secular sentiment that in the 1980s was deeply entrenched. His critics spoke for some of the most conservative strands. Their campaign against *The Satanic Verses* was not to protect Muslim communities from unconscionable attack from anti-Muslim bigots but, rather, to protect their own privileged position within those communities from political assault from radical critics, to assert their right to be the true voice of Islam by denying legitimacy to such critics. And they succeeded at least in part because secular liberals embraced them as the 'authentic' voice of the Muslim community.

The Satanic Verses was published in September 1988. For the next five months, until Ayatollah Khomeini issued his fatwa on Valentine's Day 1989, most Muslims ignored the book. The campaign against the novel

was largely confined to the Indian subcontinent and the UK. Aside from the involvement
of Saudi Arabia, there was little enthusiasm
for any campaign against the novel in the
Arab world or in Turkey, or among Muslim
communities in France or Germany. When
the Saudi authorities tried at the end of 1988
to get the novel banned in Muslim countries
worldwide, few responded except those with
large subcontinental populations. Even in
Iran, the book was openly available and was
reviewed in many newspapers.

As in the controversy over the Danish
cartoons, it was politics, not religion, that
transformed *The Satanic Verses* into a worldwide event of historic proportions. The novel
first became an issue in India because the
Jamaat-e-Islami, an Islamist group against
which Rushdie had taken aim in his previous
novel *Shame* (1983), tried to use the novel as
political leverage in a general-election campaign. From India, the anti-Rushdie campaign spilt into the UK, where the Jamaat

had a network of organizations funded by the Saudi government. From 1970s onwards, Saudi Arabia had used oil money to fund Salafi organizations and mosques worldwide to cement its position as spokesman for the *umma*. Then came the Iranian Revolution of 1979 that overthrew the shah, established an Islamic republic, made Tehran the capital of Muslim radicalism and Ayatollah Khomeini its spiritual leader, and posed a direct challenge to Riyadh. *The Satanic Verses* became a weapon in that conflict between Saudi Arabia and Iran. Riyadh made the initial running. The fatwa was an attempt by Iran to wrestle back the initiative.

The controversy over *The Satanic Verses* was primarily a political, not a religious, conflict. But having accepted the myths that the controversy was driven by theology and that all Muslims were offended by the novel, many liberals came to the conclusion in the post-Rushdie world that the Islamists were the true voice of Islam and that in a plural society, social harmony required greater restraints on free speech.

Like Abu Laban, Rushdie's critics were seen as authentic Muslims while Rushdie, like Khader, was regarded as too Westernized, secular and progressive to be truly of his community. The same was true of Bhatti, Kureishi, Hera and countless others. Once again we see how the multicultural approach denies the diversity within minority communities. Consequently, the most conservative voices are often seen as the most authentic representatives of those communities while the progressive voices get marginalized.

Those who insist that in a plural society speech must necessarily be less free in order to protect cultural sensibilities and avoid conflicts, look at the issue back-to-front. It is precisely because we *do* live in a plural society that we need the fullest extension possible of free speech. In a homogeneous society in which everyone thought in exactly the same way, the giving of offence would be nothing more than gratuitous. But in the real world, where societies are plural, it is both inevitable and important that people offend the sensibilities of others. It is inevitable because where different beliefs are deeply held, clashes are unavoidable. Almost by definition, such clashes express what it is to live in a diverse society. And so they should be openly resolved rather than suppressed in the name of 'respect' or 'tolerance'.

More importantly, the giving of offence is not just inevitable, it is also important. Any kind of social change or social progress means offending some deeply held sensibilities. Or to put it another way: 'You can't say that!' is all too often the response of those in power to having their power challenged. To accept that certain things cannot be said is to accept that certain forms of power cannot be challenged. Human beings, as Rushdie puts it, 'shape their futures by arguing and challenging and saying the unsayable; not by bowing their knee whether to gods or to men'.[47]

The notion of giving offence suggests that certain beliefs are so important or valuable to certain people that they should be put beyond the possibility of being insulted, caricatured or even questioned. The importance of the principle of free speech lies precisely in that it provides a permanent challenge to the idea that some questions are beyond contention and hence acts as a permanent challenge to authority. This is why free speech is essential not simply to the practice of democracy but also to the aspirations of those groups who may have been failed by the formal democratic processes: to those whose voices may have been silenced by racism, for instance. The real value of free speech, in other words, is not to those who possess power but to those who want to challenge them. And the real value of censorship is to those who do not wish their authority to be challenged. The right to 'subject each others' fundamental beliefs to criticism' is the bedrock of an open, diverse society. Once we give up such a right in the

name of 'tolerance' or 'respect', we constrain
our ability to challenge those in power, and
therefore to challenge injustice.

11

Having explored the problems of multiculturalism, I want now to turn my attention to
its critics, most of whose arguments I also dis-
agree with. Much of the contemporary criticism of multiculturalism is driven by racism,
bigotry and sheer hatred for the Other.
Nowhere is this more savagely evident than
in the case of Anders Behring Breivik, the
Norwegian mass murderer.

Faced with a monster like Breivik, many
feel that we have no choice but to close ranks
and to defend that which he wishes to destroy.
It is a version of an argument that has gained
ground in recent years as populist politicians,
such as the Netherlands' Geert Wilders, and
far-right parties, such as the France's Front
National, have exploited discontent about

immigration, and as mainstream right-wing leaders, from Merkel to Cameron to Sarkozy, have become fiercer in their criticism of multiculturalism. The 'closing ranks' argument misunderstands, however, both the nature of multiculturalism and the essence of the right's criticism and, indeed, of Breivik's hatred. The real target of their hostility is not so much multiculturalism as immigrants, immigration and diversity. And to challenge anti-immigration hostility and opposition to diversity we need also to challenge multiculturalism.

Underpinning the right-wing assault on multiculturalism is the 'clash of civilizations' thesis. The phrase was coined by British historian Bernard Lewis in his 1990 essay 'The Roots of Muslim Rage' and subsequently popularized by the American political scientist Samuel Huntington. The conflicts that had convulsed Europe over the past centuries, Huntington wrote, from the wars of religion between Protestants and Catholics to the Cold War, were all 'conflicts within Western civilization'.[48] The 'battle lines of the future',[49] on the other hand, would be *between* civilizations. And the most deep-set of these would be between the Christian West and the Islamic East, which would be 'far more fundamental' than any war unleashed by 'differences among political ideologies and political regimes'.[50] The West would need vigorously to defend its values and beliefs against Islamic assault.

It is an argument that has gained an increasing hearing in the wake of 9/11. 'All over again,' British novelist Martin Amis wrote, 'the West confronts an irrationalist, agonistic, theocratic/ideocratic system which is essentially unappeasably opposed to its existence.'[51] Islam, claimed Canadian journalist Mark Steyn, 'is not just a religion. There's a global *jihad* lurking within this religion' which is 'a bloodthirsty faith in which whatever's your bag violence-wise can almost certainly be justified'.[52] 'At the end of the

Middle Ages,' Cardinal Miloslav Vlk, the archbishop of Prague, has observed, 'Islam failed to conquer Europe with arms.' Today, though, 'the fall of Europe is looming.'[53]

In this climate of existential fear, immigration has come to be seen as a Trojan Horse for the destruction of European civilization. 'Demographically,' Thilo Sarrazin, a prominent German banker and senior figure in the Social Democratic Party, wrote in his 2010 book *Deutschland schafft sich ab* (Germany Abolishes Itself), 'the enormous fertility of Muslim migrants is a threat to the cultural and civilizational equilibrium of an ageing Europe.'[54] A succession of books in recent years by authors such as Bruce Bawer, Melanie Phillips, Mark Steyn, Italian writer Oriana Fallaci and American author Christopher Caldwell have warned that immigration, in particular Muslim immigration, is threatening the very foundations of European civilization. 'Imagine that the West, at the height of the Cold War, had received a mass influx of immigrants from Communist countries who were ambivalent about which side they supported,' Caldwell suggests. 'Something similar is taking place now.'[55]

Caldwell's *Reflections on the Revolution in Europe* (2009) has been perhaps the most influential of the anti-immigration critiques, garnering high praise not only from right-wing critics of immigration but also from many liberals. A columnist for the *Financial Times* and an editor of the conservative American magazine the *Weekly Standard*, the title of Caldwell's book is a nod to Edmund Burke's 1790 *Reflections on the Revolution in France*, a broadside against the French Revolution, and reflects his belief that the impact on Europe of post-war immigration has been as dramatic as the fall of the French *ancien régime* in 1789.

Two basic arguments underlie Caldwell's thesis. First, post-war immigration to Europe has, he believes, been fundamentally different from previous waves of immigration. And, second, he insists that the values of Islam are fundamentally different to those of the West, rendering Muslim migration akin to a form of colonization, tearing at the very fabric of European societies.

Prior to the Second World War, he argues, immigrants came almost exclusively from other European nations and, so, were easily assimilable. Indeed, he insists, 'using the word immigration to describe intra-European movements makes only slightly more sense than describing a New Yorker as an "immigrant" to California.' Pre-war immigration between European nations was different from post-war immigration from outside Europe because 'immigration from neighbouring countries does not provoke the most worrisome immigration questions, such as "How well will they fit in?" "Is assimilation what they want?" and, most of all, "Where are their true loyalties?" '[56]

In fact, those were the very questions asked of European migrants, on both sides of the Atlantic, in the pre-war years. A century

before the fears of the Muslim tide over-
whelming Western civilization, the same
fears were expressed about the Catholic tide.
Catholicism, as Dutch historian Leo Lucassen
observes, was perceived in the US as 'repre-
senting an entirely different culture and
worldview, and it was feared because of the
faith's global and expansive aspirations'.[57] 'It
is the political character of the Roman
Church,' wrote American author Ralph Waldo
Emerson, 'that makes it incompatible with our
institutions & unwelcome here.'[58]

After the Catholic invasion came the Jewish invasion. The UK's first immigration law,
the 1905 Aliens Act, was designed primarily
to bar European Jews, who were seen as un-
British. The then prime minister Arthur Balfour observed that without such a law, 'though
the Briton of the future might have the same
laws, the same institutions and constitution
[. . .] nationality would not be the same
and would not be the nationality we should
desire to be our heirs through the ages yet to

come.'[59] Two years earlier, the British Royal Commission on Alien Immigration had expressed fears that newcomers were inclined to live 'according to their traditions, usages and customs' and there were fears that they might be 'grafted onto the English stock [. . .] the debilitated sickly and vicious products of Europe'.[60]

It was not simply Catholics or Jews that were treated as alien invaders. In France, nearly one-third of the population in the 1930s were immigrants, mostly from Southern Europe. Today we think of Italian or Portuguese migrants as culturally similar to their French hosts. Seventy years ago, they were viewed as aliens, given to crime and violence, and unlikely to assimilate into French society. 'The notion of the easy assimilation of past European immigrants,' French historian Maxim Silverman has written, 'is a myth.'[61] One of the consequences of post-war migration has been the creation of historical amnesia about pre-war attitudes as well as about the divided nature of European societies before such immigration. From a historical perspective, there is little that is unique about contemporary migrants or in the way that host societies perceive them.

Caldwell's second major theme is that '[s]ince its arrival half a century ago, Islam has broken—or required adjustments to, or rearguard defenses of—a good many of the European customs, received ideas and state structures with which it has come in contact.'[62] Islam, he insists, 'is not enhancing or validating European culture; it is supplanting it'.[63]

Historically, we have seen that this is not so. In the 1960s and 70s, Muslim immigrants did not yearn to express their differences but, rather, demanded that they not be treated differently. Only subsequently did Muslims, from a generation that was ironically far more integrated than that of their parents, begin to assert their cultural distinctiveness. This is the paradox of immigration and integration that few academics or policy-makers have been willing to address or even acknowledge.

In any case, even as he promotes the idea, drawn from Huntington, of the radical rupture between Islamic and Western civilizations, Caldwell reveals the inadequacies of this way of thinking. 'What secular Europeans call "Islam",' he points out, 'is a set of values that Dante and Erasmus would recognize as theirs.' On the other hand, the modern, secular rights that now constitute 'core European values' would 'leave Dante and Erasmus bewildered'.[64] There is, in other words, no single set of European values that transcends history in opposition to a single corpus of timeless set-in-stone Islamic values. This is the fundamental problem with the clash of civilizations thesis: a blindness to historical change, to the complexities of culture and the interwovenness of cultural engagement. The values of both European and Islamic societies have transformed dramatically over the past millennium, partly through conversations with each other. It was the Islamic empire, for instance, which helped preserve the ancient Greek philosophical tradition and it was primarily through the Islamic Empire that scholars in Western Europe rediscovered that tradition at the turn of the last millennium. Ironically, Islamic scholarship helped transform Christian cultures much more than it did Muslim cultures and eventually to create the gulf between the West and Islam that allows many to talk about the 'clash of civilizations'.

What is striking is that many of the arguments of right-wing critics of multiculturalism who draw upon the clash of civilizations thesis are similar to those of multiculturalists. It is true that there is little love lost between the two groups. Multiculturalists accuse clash of civilizations warriors of pandering to racism and Islamophobia; clash of civilizations warriors charge multiculturalists with appeasing Islamism. Beneath the hostility, however, the two sides share basic assumptions about the nature of culture, identity and difference. Both view the key social divisions as cultural or civilizational. Both see cultures, or civilizations, as homogeneous entities. Both insist on the crucial importance of cultural identity and on the preservation of such identity. Both perceive irresolvable conflicts arising from incommensurate values.

Even the language crosses the divide. At the heart of the populist assault on multiculturalism is a defence of 'my culture', 'my history', 'my tradition'. Listen, for instance, to the language that Breivik employed at his trial. Multiculturalism, he claimed, is a 'hate ideology'. He lamented its 'deconstruction of European cultures and traditions', and saw himself as acting 'in defence of my culture and of my people'.[65] This is precisely the language of culture and identity that multiculturalism has done so much to foster in recent years.

12

Martin Amis has written that 9/11 was 'a day of de-Enlightenment'[66]—a theocratic assault on liberal democratic traditions and on a secular, rationalist culture. Re-Enlightening the world requires us to engage in a civilizational war. For many, the clash of civilizations argument provides a necessary defence of Enlightenment values.

Yet, in the writings of such liberals, the Enlightenment often seems less like a set of values through which to create a progressive politics than a myth by which to define the West. As much as multiculturalism, the clash of civilizations thesis has signalled an abandonment by liberals of basic liberal values. 'One of the main claims of Enlightenment philosophy,' Dutch writer Ian Buruma observes in *Murder in Amsterdam* (2006), his meditation on the significance of the killing of Dutch filmmaker Theo van Gogh by a Moroccan Islamist, 'is that its ideas based on reason are by definition universal. But the

Enlightenment has a particular appeal to some [. . .] because its values are not just universal, but more importantly "ours", that is European, Western values.'[67]

In the same vein, American writer Sam Harris has suggested that Islam is such an alien force that different rules must apply to the way Muslims are treated. Harris has made a liberal case for torture, arguing that 'if we are willing to drop bombs or even risk that pistol rounds might go astray, we should be willing to torture a certain class of criminal suspect and military prisoners.'[68] Since most terrorists are Muslim, there is, he argues, a need for ethnic profiling and discriminatory policing. He also believes that 'some propositions are so dangerous that it may even be ethical to kill people for believing them.'[69] Harris has even written that 'The people who speak most sensibly about the threat that Islam poses to Europe are actually fascists.'[70]

Amis admitted in an interview in the London *Times*

a definite urge [. . .] to say that 'The
Muslim community will have to suf-
fer until it gets its house in order.'
What sort of suffering? Not let them
travel. Deportation—further down
the road. Curtailing of freedoms.
Strip-searching people who look like
they're from the Middle East or from
Pakistan [. . .] Discriminatory stuff,
until it hurts the whole community
and they start getting tough with
their children.[71]

He was, Amis argued later, merely
engaging in a 'thought experiment'; but it
was a thought experiment that revealed
much about how Muslims are, for many liberals today, the 'Other'.

Once the Enlightenment becomes a
weapon in the clash of civilizations rather than
in the battle to define the values and attitudes
necessary to advance political rights and social
justice, once it becomes a measure as much of
tribal attachment as of progressive politics,

then everything from torture to collective punishment becomes permissible and the pursuit of Enlightenment itself becomes a source of de-Enlightenment.

'For are they not conjoined opposites, these two, each man the other's shadow?'[72] asks Rushdie in *The Satanic Verses* about his two anti-heroes, Saladin Chamcha and Gibreel Farishta. One might ask the same question about the multiculturalist argument and the clash of civilizations thesis. These two responses to diversity appear as conjoined opposites, each as the other's shadow, each betraying fundamental liberal principles. One abandons the basic Enlightenment idea of universal values, suggesting instead that we should accept that every society is a collection of disparate communities and that social harmony requires greater censorship and less freedom. The other turns belief in the Enlightenment into a tribal affair: Enlightenment values are good because they are ours and we should militantly defend our values and lifestyles, even to the extent of denying such values and lifestyles to others. Or, as Rushdie says about Saladin and Gibreel, 'One seeking to transform into the foreignness he admires, the other seeking contemptuously to transform.'[73]

When we say that we live in a diverse society, what we mean is that it is a messy world out there full of clashes and conflicts. And that is all for the good, for it is out of such clashes and conflicts that cultural and political engagement emerges. Or, to put it another way, diversity is important, not in and of itself but because it allows us to break out of our culture-bound boxes, by engaging in dialogue and debate and by putting different values, beliefs and lifestyles to the test. But the very thing that is valuable about diversity—the cultural and ideological clashes that it brings about—is also the very thing that many people fear. That fear takes two forms. On the one hand is the dread of the Other, a sense that immigration is undermining the national fabric, eroding the continuity of history and culture, undermining Western values. On the other is the multicultural belief that diversity has to be policed to minimize the clashes and conflicts and frictions that it brings in its wake, that everything has to be nicely parcelled up into pigeonholes of cultures and ethnicities and faiths, the messiness neat and ordered. These are the Saladin Chamchas and the Gibreel Farishtas of the contemporary world. It is time we rejected both. It is time we rebuffed both multiculturalism and its discontents. It is time we stopped fearing the messiness of the world and started seeing it as the raw material of social engagement, the bricks and the mortar of social renewal.

Notes

1 Anders Behring Breivik, *2083: A European Declaration of Independence*, p. 1111. Available at: http://publicintelligence.net/anders-behring-breiviks-complete-manifesto-2083-a-

european-declaration-of-independence/ (last accessed on 23 August 2013).

2 Bruce Bawer, 'Inside the Mind of the Oslo Murderer', *Wall Street Journal* (25 July 2011).

3 Melanie Phillips, 'Hatred, Smears and the Liberals Hell-Bent on Bullying Millions of Us into Silence', *Daily Mail* (1 August 2011).

4 David Hume, *An Enquiry Concerning Human Understanding* (Peter Millican ed.) (Oxford and New York: Oxford University Press, 2007), p. 60.

5 Johann Gottfried Herder, *Outlines of a Philosophy of the History of Man*, VOL. 2 (T. O. Churchill trans.) (London: Luke Hansard, 1803), p. 272.

6 Charles Taylor, 'The Politics of Recognition' in Charles Taylor, *Multiculturalism*: *Examining the Politics of Recognition* (Amy Gutman ed. and introd.) (Princeton, NJ: Princeton University Press, 1994), pp. 25–73; here, p. 30.

7 Ibid., p. 31.

8 Ibid., p. 28.

9   Stuart Hall, 'The Question of Cultural Identity' in Stuart Hall, David Held and Tony McGrew (eds), *Modernity and its Futures*: *Understanding Modern Societies* (Cambridge: Polity Press, 1992), pp. 273–326; here, p. 277.

10 John Gray, *Two Faces of Liberalism* (New York: New Press, 2002), p. 121.

11 Taylor, 'The Politics of Recognition', p. 31.

12 Will Kymlicka, *Multicultural Citizenship*: *A Liberal Theory of Minority Rights* (Oxford and New York: Oxford University Press, 1992), p. 47.

13 Bhikhu Parekh, 'Superior Peoples: The Narrowness of Liberalism from Mill to Rawls', *Times Literary Supplement* (25 February 1994), pp. 11–13; here, p. 13.

14 Tariq Modood, 'Introduction: The Politics of Multiculturalism in the New Europe' in Tariq Modood and Pnina Werbner (eds), *The Politics of Multiculturalism in the New Europe* (London: Zed Books, 1997), pp. 1–26; here, pp. 19–20.

15 Iris Marion Young, *Justice and the Politics of Difference* (Princeton, NJ: Princeton University Press, 1990), p. 174.

16 Taylor, 'The Politics of Recognition', p. 41.

17 Joseph Raz, *Ethics in the Public Domain*: *Essays in the Morality of Law and Politics* (Oxford: Oxford University Press, 1995), p. 162.

18 Avishai Margalit and Joseph Raz, 'National Self-Determination', *Journal of Philosophy* 87(9) (September 1990): 439–61; here, p. 449.

19 Kymlicka, *Multicultural Citizenship*, p. 83.

20 Taylor, 'The Politics of Recognition', p. 40.

21 Kymlicka, *Multicultural Citizenship*, p. 104.

22 Richard Wright, 'I Bite the Hand that Feeds Me', *Atlantic Monthly* 155 (June 1940): 826–8; here, p. 828.

23 Ibid., 827.

24 Walter Benn Michaels, *Our America*: *Nativism, Modernism and Pluralism* (Durham, NC: Duke University Press, 1995), pp. 120–1.

25 Kwame Anthony Appiah, *The Ethics of Identity* (Princeton, NJ: Princeton University Press, 2010), p. 117.

26 See David A. Hollinger, *Postethnic America*: *Beyond Multiculturalism* (New York: Basic Books, 1995), p. 152.

27 Dennis Wrong, 'Cultural Relativism as Ideology', *Critical Review* 11(2) (1997): 291–300; here, p. 299.

28 Philippe Buchez, 'Rapport fait à la Société medico-psyhologique sur le *Traité des dégénérescences physiques, intellectuelles, et morales de l'espèce humaine et des causes qui les produisent*', *Annales medico-psychologique* 3 (1857): 455–67; here, p. 462 (my translation).

29 'Slaves and Labourers', *Saturday Review* 17 (1864).

30 PRO/CO 1028/22, 'Working Party on Coloured People Seeking Employment in the United Kingdom: Draft Report', 28 October 1953.

31 Pervaiz Khan, interview with the author, 20 October 2008; see also Kenan Malik, *From Fatwa to Jihad: The Rushdie Affair and Its Legacy* (London: Atlantic Books, 2009), pp. 46–7, 67–8, 101–2.

32 Quoted in Gilles Kepel, *Les Banlieus d'Islam* (Paris: Seuil, 1991), p. 140 (my translation).

33 Ibid., p. 17 (my translation).

34 Quoted in John Rex and Sally Tomlinson, *Colonial Immigrants in a British City*: *A Class Analysis* (London: Routledge, 1979), p. 170.

35 Quoted in Robert Miles and Annie Phizacklea, *White Man's Country*: *Racism in British Politics* (London: Pluto, 1984), p. 62.

36 Darcus Howe, *From Bobby to Babylon*: *Blacks and the British Police* (London: Race Today Publications, 1988), p. 52.

37 Bhikhu Parekh, preface to *The Future of Multi-ethnic Britain*: *The Parekh Report* (London: Profile Books, 2000), p. ix.

38 Oliver Decker, Marliese Weissmann, Johannes Kiess and Elmar Brähler, *Die Mitte in Der Krise*: *Rechtsextreme Einstellungen in Deutschland 2010* (Berlin: Friedrich-Ebert-Stiftung, 2010).

39 Birmingham City Council, *Joint Report of Head of Equalities and Director of Birmingham Race Action Partnership*: *Development of Issue-Based Community Action Forums* (Birmingham: Birmingham City Council, 1999), p. 4.

40 See Graham Smith and Susan Stephenson, 'The Theory and Practice of Group

Representation: Reflections on the Politics of Race Equality in Birmingham', *Public Administration* 83(2) (1995): 323–43.

41 Joy Warmington, interview with the author, 21 November 2005; see also Malik, *From Fatwa to Jihad*, pp. 68–9.

42 See Amartya Sen, 'The Uses and Abuses of Multiculturalism: Chili and Liberty', *New Republic* (27 February 2006): 25–9.

43 Nasser Khader, interview with the author, 29 September 2008; see also Malik, *From Fatwa to Jihad*, pp. 163–5.

44 'See No Evil: Interview with Jytte Klausen', *Index on Censorship* 28(4) (18 December 2009): 74–80. Available at: http://www.indexoncensorship.org/-2009/12/from-the-magazine-see-no-evil/ (last accessed on 13 September 2013).

45 Khader, interview with the author, 29 September 2008.

46 Tariq Modood, 'Multiculturalism, Secularism and the State' in Richard Bellamy and Martin Hollis (eds), *Pluralism and Liberal Neutrality* (Ilford, Essex and Portland, OR: Frank Cass Publishers), pp. 79–97; here, p. 93.

47 Salman Rushdie, *In Good Faith* (London: Granta, 1990), p. 4.

48 Samuel P. Huntington, 'The Clash of Civilizations', *Foreign Affairs* (Summer 1993): 22–49; here, p. 23.

49 Ibid., p. 22.

50 Ibid., p. 25.

51 Martin Amis, 'Fear and Loathing', *Guardian* (18 September 2001).

52 Mark Steyn, *America Alone: The End of the World As We Know It* (Washington: Regnery Publishing, 2006), p. 62.

53 Quoted in Riazat Butt, 'Vatican Cardinal Blames Christians over "Islamisation" of Europe', *Guardian* (7 January 2010).

54 Thilo Sarrazin, cited in Doug Saunders, *The Myth of the Muslim Tide: Do Immigrants Threaten the West?* (New York: Vintage, 2012), p. 27.

55 Christopher Caldwell, *Reflections on the Revolution in Europe: Immigration, Islam and the West* (London: Anchor Books, 2010), p. 132.

56 Ibid., p. 9.

57 Leo Lucassen, *The Immigrant Threat: The Integration of Old And New Migrants in Western Europe since 1850* (Champaign: The University of Illinois Press, 2005), p. 22.

58 Quoted in Saunders, *The Myth of the Muslim Tide*, p. 122.

59 Quoted in Brian Klug, 'The Other Arthur Balfour: "Protector of the Jews"', The Balfour Project. Available at: http://www.balfourproject.org/the-other-arthur-balfour-protector-of-the-jews/ (last accessed on 27 August 2013).

60 James Silver, quoted in *Eastern Post* (2 November 1901), cited in Steve Cohen, *No One Is Illegal: Asylum and Immigration Control Past and Present* (Stoke-on-Trent, Staffordshire: Trentham Books, 2003), p. 87.

61 Maxim Silverman, *Deconstructing the Nation: Immigration, Racism and Citizenship in Modern France* (London: Routledge, 1992), p. 81.

62 Caldwell, *Reflections on the Revolution in Europe*, p. 11.

63 Ibid., p. 17.

64 Ibid., p. 197.

65 Quoted in Brendan O'Neil, 'Breivik: A Monster Made by Multiculturalism', *Telegraph* (18 April 2012).

66 Martin Amis, 'The Voice of the Lonely Crowd', *Guardian* (1 June 2002).

67 Ian Buruma, *Murder in Amsterdam: The Death of Theo van Gogh and the Limits of Tolerance* (London and New York: Penguin Books, 2010), p. 29.

68 Sam Harris, *The End of Faith: Religion, Terror and the Future of Reason* (New York: W. W. Norton, 2005), p. 197.

69 Ibid., p. 52.

70 Sam Harris, 'It's Real. It's Scary. It's a Cult of Death', *Los Angeles Times* (18 September 2006).

71 Ginny Dougary, 'The Voice of Experience', Interview with Martin Amis, *Times Online* (9 September 2006). Available at: http://www.ginnydougary.co.uk/2006/09/17/the-voice-of-experience/ (last accessed on 27 August 2013).

72 Salman Rushdie, *The Satanic Verses* (New York: Viking, 1989), p. 426.

73 Ibid.